Meet a Genius

Rob Alcraft

Explorer Challenge

Find out which genius had
a badly behaved dog...

OXFORD
UNIVERSITY PRESS

Contents

The Wonder Child 5

The Woman Who Changed Science 13

The Man Who Dreamed of Numbers ... 21

Being a Genius Is Simple! 29

Glossary and Index 30

Look Back, Explorers 31

A genius is a person with an extraordinary ability. They can do things that other people can't do.

Come and find out some weird and wonderful facts about three geniuses.

Which genius wore her wedding dress to work?

Which genius failed most of his exams?

Which genius was scared of trumpets?

The Wonder Child

Wolfgang Amadeus Mozart
(*say* wolf-gang am-a-day-us moat-sart)

Mozart was a musical genius.

He began to **compose**
music at the age of five.

- Born 1756, in Austria

- Composed over 600 pieces of music

- Died aged 35

Mozart was a child star. He went all over Europe with his sister and father, and played concerts for kings and queens.

Mozart could play the harpsichord from the age of four.

Mozart never went to school – his dad taught him at home.

He wrote his first **symphony** when he was eight.

Mozart wore pigtails. For concerts, he wore fashionable white wigs.

Mozart loved:
dumplings,
his wife Constanze –
and his hair too!

Liver dumplings were
his favourite food.

He married Constanze in 1782.

He had his hair
styled every day.

And he loved me!

Mozart taught some of his
own music to his pet starling.

Mozart hated:

trumpets,
Paris –
and being told what to do!

He was afraid of trumpets – they made him cry!

Mozart hated being told what to do. He argued so much that he once lost his job!

He thought that Paris was dirty.

Mozart thought that he and his son had weird ears. He made this drawing to prove it!

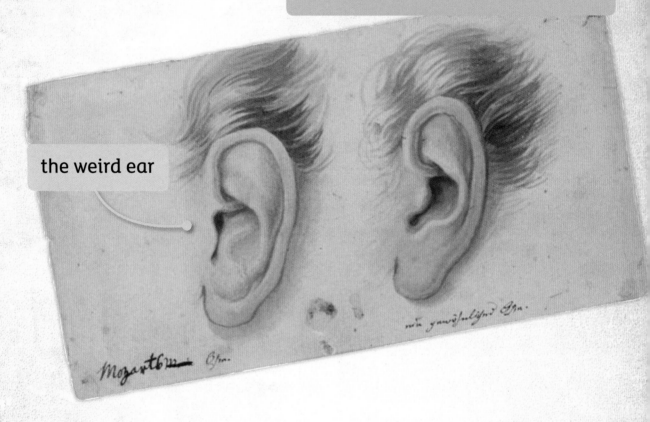

the weird ear

Mozart composed music in his head, sometimes scribbling notes as he went along. He said he thought about music all day long.

It was hard work being a genius. Mozart once wrote 'nobody has devoted so much time and thought to music as I'.

He had to travel for work a lot.
Mozart spent 3720 days on the road.
That's over 10 years of travel!

 Genius!

Mozart is one of the most famous composers ever.

Every year thousands of people come to Mozart's home town for a music festival celebrating his work.

Greatest Work

The Magic Flute is an **opera** by Mozart. It's still so popular that it is performed over 500 times a year around the world!

The Woman Who Changed Science

Marie Curie
(*say* ma-ree cure-ee)

Curie was a science genius.

Her discoveries about **radiation** changed science for ever.

- Born 1867, in Poland

- Won two **Nobel Prizes** for her discoveries in science

- Died aged 66

She taught herself to read aged four.

Curie

sisters

father

When Curie's mother died, her father had to take in **lodgers** to pay the bills. Curie had to sleep on the floor!

Her dad was a science teacher.

Curie was a brilliant student,
but girls weren't allowed to
go to university in Poland
when she was young.

Instead, Curie studied
in secret classes.

She worked for seven years
as a **governess**. When Curie had
saved enough money, she moved to
France to study at a university in Paris.

Curie loved:

books,
hot chocolate –
and Pierre!

bonjour *hello* *здравствуйте* *guten Tag* *cześć*

Français
Deutsch
русский
English
Polski

She read books in
five languages.

When she was a student
she survived on hot
chocolate, bread and fruit.

**She loved
me too!**

Her family's dog,
Lancet, was big
and badly behaved.

She married Pierre in 1895.
He was a scientist too.

Curie hated:

learning Russian history,
being a governess –
and not sharing!

She didn't like learning Russian history.

She only worked as a governess so she could save money to study.

She preferred to share her science ideas, rather than make money from them.

When Marie and Pierre got married, they were poor.

They had to work in a leaky shed instead of a laboratory, and Curie wore her old wedding dress for work!

Curie worked hard for a long time to find out about radiation. She discovered a new metal that no one had known about, called radium.

The metal gave off a strange energy that Curie called radioactivity.

After dark the Curies' shed was filled with a blue-green glow. The glow came from radiation.

!
Danger

Curie's notebooks are so radioactive that it is dangerous to touch them.

Curie was the first person ever to win two Nobel Prizes for science.

At the time, some people thought women should not work in science. Her success showed that women could be scientists and she led the way for other women to study science.

Greatest Work

Curie's work proved it was possible to split an **atom**.

The Man Who Dreamed of Numbers

Srinivasa Ramanujan
(*say* sree-nee-va-sa ra-man-oo-jan)

Ramanujan had one of the greatest maths brains ever.

He said that sometimes he got the answers to maths puzzles in his dreams.

- Born 1887, in India

- Taught himself maths and thought up thousands of new maths ideas

- Died aged 32

mother

Ramanujan

Ramanujan was a genius
at maths – but he wouldn't study
anything else.

He failed all his college exams –
except maths of course! In one exam
Ramanujan didn't answer a single question.

Ramanujan worked
outside his house.

Ramanujan invented his
own maths language to write
down his ideas.

He started out writing on
a slate using chalk, and
rubbed out with his elbow.

Ramanujan loved:

notebooks,
numbers –
and talking!

He filled notebooks with maths answers.

Someone who knew him wrote that every number was his personal friend.

$6.67408 \times 10^{-11}\ m^3\ kg^{-1}\ s^{-2}$

He loved me too!

A friend once had to throw a pot of water over his head to stop him talking!

When he had a job in England, Ramanujan wrote home asking for coconut oil.

Ramanujan hated:

leaving his home in India,
English shoes –
and English weather!

When he was first asked
to come to England,
Ramanujan refused to go.

He didn't like English
shoes, so he wore slippers
instead – even outside!

The English weather
made him miserable.

These are pages from Ramanujan's notebooks.

Ramanujan's ideas were difficult and new. Hardly anyone understood them.

Almost no one understood this either!

Ramanujan worked at Cambridge University. He was often unhappy as he missed home, but still came up with amazing new maths ideas.

At home, Ramanujan dressed in Indian fashions. When he went to England he wore a suit for the first time.

He went punting.

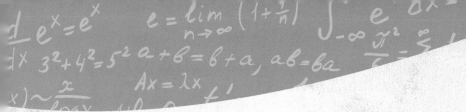

Today, Ramanujan's maths is helping scientists to work out what happens inside a **black hole** – mind-boggling!

Greatest Work

Websites use number patterns which Ramanujan worked out.

Being a Genius
Is Simple!

You've met three geniuses, so now you know their simple secrets:

- they all had extraordinary ability;
- they all loved their work;
- they all worked really hard, and never stopped.

Glossary

atom: tiny parts from which everything is made

black hole: a part of space that pulls light and things into it

compose: to make up or create

governess: a woman who teaches children in their home

harpsichord: a musical instrument like a small piano

lodgers: people who pay to live in someone's house

Nobel Prizes: prizes awarded for amazing work in science, medicine, and other subjects

opera: a drama where all the words are sung

radiation: a dangerous type of energy which comes from some materials like radium

symphony: a long piece of music for an orchestra

Index

compose	5, 10	music	5, 8, 10, 12
concerts	6, 7	Nobel Prizes	13, 20
genius	4, 5, 10, 12, 13, 20, 22, 28, 29	radiation	13, 19
ideas	17, 21, 23, 26, 27	science	13, 14, 17, 20
maths	21, 22, 23, 24, 27, 28	student	15, 16

Look Back, Explorers

How old was Mozart when he began to compose music?

Why did Curie have to study in secret classes?

The English weather made Ramanujan *miserable*. Can you think of another word that means the same as *miserable*?

Why do you think Mozart had to travel for work so much?

Why did Ramanujan write home asking for coconut oil, instead of buying it in England?

Did you find out which genius had a badly behaved dog?

What's Next, Explorers?

Now you know about three geniuses, read a story where the magic key takes Nadim to meet Mozart ...

Explorer Challenge
for *Meeting Mozart*

Find out who wrote this piece of music ...